SO-BIL-053

I Love You Enough To...
LET YOU GO

LENDING LIBRARY

UNITY OF TUCSON, INC.
3617 N. Camino Blanco
TUCSON, ARIZONA 85718-7239
(602) 577-3300

3-13

I Love You Enough To... LET YOU GO

Spiritual Contemplations
by Jim McGregor

Photography by Janie Bullard

 Willeo Publishing, Roswell, Georgia

WILLEO PUBLISHING
I Love You Enough... To Let You Go
Copyright © 1990 by Jim McGregor
Photographs © 1992 by Janie Bullard
Book Design by Alicia Macbeth Jacobs
Willeo Publishing, Publisher

All rights reserved. Printed in the United States of
America. No part of this book may be used or reproduced
in any manner whatsoever without written permission of
the publisher.
For ordering information please contact Willeo
Publishing, 530 Willeo Road, Roswell, Georgia, 30075,
(404) 992-9266 or 1-800-343-1662.

2nd Edition
ISBN 0-940549-05-0

ince it first appeared in 1983, *I Love You Enough To...Let You Go* has inspired thousands of people, many with addicted relatives or friends, to love in a healthy and freeing way. Its simple yet profound message was originally written in response to a friend who was struggling to "turn his back," as he put it, on the drug-addicted son he dearly loved.

The giver of the unconditional love described in *I Love You Enough To...Let You Go* can expect to find relief from the guilt and stress that result from assuming control and responsibility of another person's life.

Given time, the recipient of this unconditional love can find dignity, self-respect, and self-determination.

FROM THE AUTHOR

Growth is a natural flowing in which we move from that which our culture considers "normal" to peace and serenity. Fitting with this natural flow, *I Love You Enough To...Let You Go* offers a spiritual and practical approach to relationships and everyday existence.

Sometimes the need to grow comes out of hardship. Sometimes it comes from the simple awareness that things are not quite right—that there must be more to life.

Letting go is both the process and the end result of growth. To let go is to recognize and affirm the dignity and self-determining power of every individual, including one's self.

Letting go a little is a relief...for some, simple relief is enough.

Letting go a lot is freeing...venturing further, others strive to apply these principles constantly in their lives, often with the help of various programs and disciplines.

Letting go completely is bliss...achieving a universal state of being allows individuals to recognize the natural ebb and flow in all existence. Actions and decisions come to them, and they know that these actions and decisions are perfect not only for them, but for the universe as a whole.

It is my hope that *I Love You Enough To...Let You Go* will be a positive experience for you as you travel along your spiritual path.

℘

Special thanks go to my beautiful wife Phyllis, who edited my original writings and used her creative talents to make *I Love You Enough To...Let You Go* a pleasure to look at as well as to read.

Thanks to Donna Armstrong, Printed Matter, Inc., who published the 1st edition of this book. I greatly appreciate her early support and commitment to my writing.

I also greatly appreciate the editorial assistance of Deborah Kowal and Ron Kite, the book design by Alicia Macbeth Jacobs, and the inspirational photographs by Janie Bullard.

I am extremely grateful to the many people in recovery whose suggestions and positive reactions to *I Love You Enough To...Let You Go* have encouraged me over the years. I would also like to thank all those not in recovery who have accepted this book as a spiritual piece and a love poem.

Jim McGregor
Atlanta, Ga
January 1992

Contemplations

—————————— **I** ——————————

I love you

enough to…

Allow you to find the

God of your understanding

— however, whenever,

and if ever you choose.

In order to really let you go with love, I must find the serenity and peace that I believe come from a source beyond my understanding.

> It seems to me that those beautiful individuals who have found the strength and peace we all want, and who radiate love and serenity, have found a power greater than themselves.

Since I am the only person I can change, I plan to place the focus on me and keep on growing spiritually.

Only then can I allow others to find their place in the natural order of things without interference from me.

I accept your right to choose your own path to spiritual understanding whenever and if ever you choose that path.

I hope you feel the love and freedom I am sending your way.

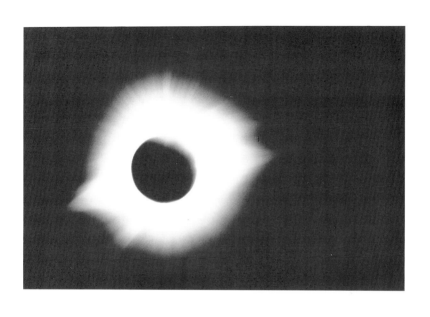

I love you

enough to...

Allow you to make

what I perceive to be

foolish mistakes.

I believe the freedom to make mistakes is often a first step to understanding the true nature of things.

The natural order is cyclical and will always continue in motion, so how can I expect to outguess these greater forces?

I have come to see mistakes as learning experiences that help me continue to grow. I love you enough to set you free, and I give you the privilege of making your own mistakes as you see fit.

I love you

enough to...

      Never possess you and

        never let you possess me.

I love you in a way that has nothing to do with possessing each other. On the contrary, the freedom that I treasure derives from the love of oneself in a spiritual sense that precludes the possession of another.

So how could I possess your soul?

You have the right to the dignity that every living thing has inherited at birth:

> to have choices and to be free of me as just another possession to be protected and firmly held.

I now choose that path to serenity and beauty, and I want the same for you.

I love you

enough to...

Allow you to maintain

your dignity and never let

you take away mine.

I believe that each of us is responsible for preserving his or her own dignity. As long as I maintain a strong spiritual sense, my dignity will never again be lost.

Dignity, like serenity, is not a thing that can be traded or stolen. It is mine if I claim it and yours if you do the same.

I now relieve you of the responsibility of preserving this treasure of mine, and I let go of any inclination to take care of yours.

I honor you and your right to your dignity.

—————————— V ——————————

I love you

enough to...

Allow you to seek help in

your own way, whenever

and wherever you choose.

---------------- ✺ ----------------

At some time during our life we come to a point where we need help—material, spiritual, mental, or physical. It seems that most of us consider this a sign of weakness. I did.

Whatever recovery I have enjoyed as a result of these experiences has arrived at a time and in a form that was not of my choosing.

Spiritual growth and strength can come out of the experiences of recovery from seemingly disastrous circumstances. It did for me.

> It seems that I had come to the point where I knew the beautiful life I had dreamed of was possible, and I became open to this gift when it was granted regardless of when or where it arrived.

Should you decide that there might be more to life than you now have, you have my love and support without my expectations or impositions.

I love you

enough to...

Leave your responsibilities

in your hands and

assume my own.

We cannot truly love each other without respecting each other. Part of respecting you is accepting that you have the right to live your life as you choose.

Of course, this right involves responsibilities. Since our concepts of each other's responsibilities invariably differ, how can we decide for each other?

True freedom and serenity involve knowing and being comfortable with one's own responsibilities. Knowing this, I must respect the rights of others to this beautiful gift.

I not only love you enough—I respect you enough to give back to you your responsibilities.

VII

I love you

enough to...

Allow you to hurt

when you choose.

There is nothing pleasant about mental or physical pain...

> therefore it is hard to believe that it can have a positive side.

I have found that pain is telling me that my mind or body is out of tune. When I decide to stop the pain, I must do whatever is necessary for the natural order to take over again.

My love for you includes your right to hurt—and to return to the natural order of things without interference from me.

> Is that not a gift of great value?

I believe that it is, and I hope you will receive it as such.

I love you

enough to...

Never apologize or

cover up for you.

There have been times when I have been ashamed of your actions or appearance, just as I have been ashamed of my own.

It seemed just as necessary to apologize for you as it did to offer some kind of an excuse for me, as preposterous as it now seems.

> You need never again be concerned about interference from me.

When I am involved with you, I promise to be straightforward about my feelings, and I shall not ask you to be responsible for my decisions when I find your behavior unacceptable.

From now on, you do not have to wonder what I have done to protect you from the effects of your actions, because I intend to give my full attention to my own life.

I now apologize for those times when I have infringed on your dignity by protecting you, because I now understand that I was really protecting myself.

I love you

enough to...

Be your best friend or

never see you again.

Friendship is a sacred gift that manifests itself in a variety of ways.

My new idea of friendship means that I can be friends with whomever I choose even if we are not close geographically, spiritually, or philosophically.

Diversity is a basic ingredient of the natural order of things, and therefore, it seems absurd that one's friends must share similarities.

Certainly our beliefs have differed in the past, and I now see no necessity for either of us to change them. This does not mean we are not friends. It simply means that our relationship now lies outside of my previous definition of friendship.

You are my friend regardless of circumstances that might arise. I hope my friendship will be of value to you.

— X —

I love you

enough to...

Miss you but not be

destroyed when we are

out of touch.

My ultimate strength comes from a source within myself, and no other human can be responsible for my happiness.

Even though the humanness of me cries out for your presence, my life goes on and the peace and serenity that have become a part of me are still here when we are out of touch.

It has not always been this way.

But time and an openness to the spiritual gifts available to all of us have made me capable of being a true friend even when we are apart.

Isn't that nice to know?

XI

I love you

enough to...

Drop all of my

expectations of you.

It is easy for me to expect you to be and do as I perceive you should.

> Isn't that ridiculous when you get right down to it?

Some of my expectations have to do with my disappointment in myself and some with my childish attitude that the world must be perfect, as I would have it.

I have no right to burden you with my expectations and my disappointments when those expectations are not fulfilled.

So let me change my expectations of you into wishes for the best for you.

There is something going on in the universe which lets me know that whatever your actions are, I can allow them to be a positive influence in my life even though I may not understand how this could be.

XII

I love you

enough to...

Become so serene

and at peace that

I don't "need" you.

Needing you is different than loving you. Needing is confining, while loving is freeing.

We each have everything we need to live fully—no one else can give it to us. So if I "need" you, it means that I am not taking care of myself, and it really has nothing to do with you.

My strength and serenity come from within and not "out there somewhere." Each of us has our own opinion as to what the source of that strength and serenity is.

Have you noticed that beauty in some people that has nothing to do with physical beauty or beautiful trappings?

Certainly these individuals need the necessities of life, but can you imagine them depending on another human for their inner strength?

I now relieve you of the burden of me. I now stand ready to be a true friend, which I have never been able to be in the past.

XIII

I love you

enough to...

Let go of anger

and jealousy.

How can I truly love you and still wrap you in the bindings of jealousy?

Love and jealousy are antagonistic. Love is freeing and beautiful—jealousy is restrictive and confining.

Most of the time my anger toward you is an outward manifestation of my fears...

and those fears are definitely
future-oriented.

Now that I have begun to live one day at a time there is no place for either of these two monsters in my life.

Can you see what a wonderful new world awaits me when fear and anger are no longer a part of my world?

XIV

I love you

enough to...

Allow you to have your

secret space and to have

my own.

True sharing and being in close touch are so beautiful that they require a special understanding that is beyond understanding.

There is, however, one ingredient that is necessary and which creates a paradox—each of us must have a secret space to call our own.

For me it is an absolute necessity for my contentment, so I am claiming a secret space for my own.

I am not hiding things from you, but instead I am asking you to trust me enough to allow me an inner quiet place that is mine and only mine.

Since I cannot decide what you need, I am simply allowing you the same privilege that I have claimed for myself, should you choose it.

XV

I love you

enough to...

Listen to you with an open

heart when I can.

Even though I would like to be receptive to your needs, there are times when it is impossible for me.

I wish it were not this way.

As important as you are to me and as much as I love you, at times I find that I cannot listen to you.

Have you not had the same experience with me?

This does not necessarily mean that you are making no sense or that what you are sharing is not important, but it is preposterous to expect two humans to be in a similar frame of mind at every instance.

What I can tell you is that I do value your thoughts and experiences and will listen when I can.

I hope that you can do the same for me, and I accept the fact that you have the choice to listen or not.

XVI

I love you

enough to...

> *Never tolerate your*
>
> *unacceptable behavior...*
>
> *Forgive your unacceptable*
>
> *behavior when and if*
>
> *I am ready.*

To tolerate is to degrade!

I choose not to tolerate anything about you because I love and respect you too much for that.

There are times when your behavior is totally unacceptable to me.

Since we are close, your actions are most important to me. For this reason I am learning to detach myself from those actions which I consider unacceptable.

Forgiveness is a part of loving, but not all of it. I can only love you partially without forgiving you.

Hopefully there will be a time when I will be able to forgive you—because forgiveness is a gift to myself.

XVII

I love you

enough to...

Allow you to grow

faster or slower than I do,

without resentment.

Growing at different rates does not necessarily mean growing apart.

It is easy to assume that it would be ideal if we share exactly the same experiences and grow together in beautiful harmony. Certainly there is nothing wrong with beautiful harmony. But there is so much in the world to be excited about. Wouldn't it be wonderful to share different experiences and risk growing at different rates?

The risk is that I see your success as a threat to me—that you are leaving me. I am sure we have both seen this situation manifest itself in others in the past.

> I now choose, whatever the risk, to share the excitement of diversity and not expect you to conform to me.

Growing is living. So let us each grow and live at our own pace.

XVIII

I love you

enough to...

Allow you to take

magnificent care of

yourself, your spirit, and

those things that are yours.

I choose the same for myself.

Our spirits soar when they are well tended.

Each of us has the capacity to nurture ourselves so we can be a useful and joyful addition to the universe.

The natural spiritual impulses of man are positive and uplifting. They contribute to the health and beauty of all when allowed to come forth.

I have chosen to open myself to all the wonderment of this universe—both inner and outer—and to particularly husband that spirit that is me.

I gladly allow you the same freedom, should you choose it.

XIX

I love you

enough to...

Allow you to become

the beautiful person

that you are.

I am positive that I was created a beautiful being, and I intend to allow myself to be that beautiful being once more.

Why I have allowed myself to stray from the path of serenity and freedom I do not know—

<blockquote>
and I finally realize I do not
have to know.
</blockquote>

I am now stepping aside so the flowering can happen. I delight in the vision of you joining in this experience, should you choose it.

XX

I love you

enough to...

Let you go.

I let you go in the spirit of
unconditional universal love.

ABOUT THE AUTHOR

Author Jim McGregor treasures the peace and serenity he has found writing and sharing inspirational messages that come to him. Jim has had a lifetime of experiences as a bomber pilot, food service manager, cattle breeder, financial salesman and more. The simple life he values evolved out of a year he spent in the mountains simply reflecting and meditating.

Jim's writings are influenced by his long-term involvement in a 12-step recovery program and his attachment to Eastern philosophies. His most recent work, *The Tao of Recovery*, was published by Bantam Books, January 1992.

Jim lives with his wife, Phyllis, in their home in the woods near Atlanta, Georgia. Phyllis describes Jim as a "superbly simple being with a light touch and a joyful sense of humor."